Learn to Write
Sight Words

LEARN TO WRITE
Sight Words

A Workbook for Kids

HAYLEY LEWALLEN

Illustrations by Joel and Ashley Selby

ROCKRIDGE
PRESS

For general information on our other products and services or to obtain technical support, please contact our Customer Care Department within the United States at (866) 744-2665, or outside the United States at (510) 253-0500.

Rockridge Press publishes its books in a variety of electronic and print formats. Some content that appears in print may not be available in electronic books, and vice versa.

Interior and Cover Designer: Liz Cosgrove
Art Producer: Samantha Ulban
Editor: Alyson Penn
Production Editor: Jenna Dutton

Illustrations © 2020 Joel and Ashley Selby
All other illustrations used under license
© Shutterstock

ISBN: Print 978-1-64611-924-0

R0

Note to Parents

I am thrilled that you and your child have chosen to work on writing sight words! Sight words are the foundation of reading and writing, and will help your child learn to read and write with fluency. Sight words are high-frequency words that children should be able to recognize by sight only, not by sounding them out. Your child will see these words more than any others as they read and write, so it is important that they can recognize and write them.

The words in this book have been selected from Dolch word lists and Fry word lists, geared toward children five to seven years old. I have carefully chosen 100 sight words that I believe are the foundation of your child's reading and writing skills. Your child will begin by writing two-letter sight words, and work their way up to words with six letters. They may not be able to read the words or sentences independently yet, but you can guide them using the provided pictures.

I am a former kindergarten teacher and an expert in teaching sight words and helping students become better readers and writers. I love to feature sight-words resources and other fun activities on my website, ThePrimaryPost.com.

As a current stay-at-home mom, I understand the importance of having resources like this workbook available to help your child outside of school. As your child works on each word, please encourage them to have fun and enjoy writing! I have provided extension activities at the bottom of each page to help make the exercises more engaging.

I hope you and your child enjoy writing your way through each word!

Let's get started!
Hayley Lewallen

Let's get started!

we

Say it, then trace it!

1 2 3 4

We we we we we we

we we we we we we

Write the word.

We we We We

Trace the word in the sentence.

We ride the bus.

Write the word and trace the sentence.

We ride the bus.

Write the sentence on your own!

  Can you write this word in the air with your finger?

go

Say it, then trace it!

Write the word.

Trace the word in the sentence.

The car can go fast.

Write the word and trace the sentence.

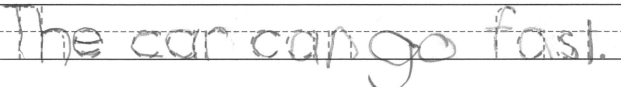

Write the sentence on your own!

 Can you think of another sentence using this word?

3

my

Say it, then trace it!

1 2→3   1   2
my my my my my my
my my my my my

Write the word.

my my my my my my

Trace the word in the sentence.

My cat likes to sit.

Write the word and trace the sentence.

cat likes to sit.

Write the sentence on your own!

MY cat likes tsil.

Spell this word out loud. Clap each time you say a letter.

at

Say it, then trace it!

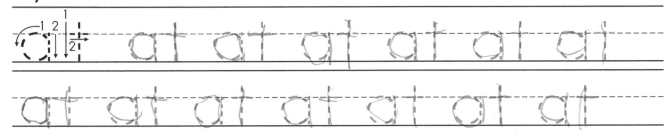

at at at at at at at at at at at at at at

Write the word.

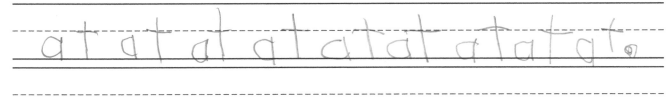

at at at at at at at at at at at at

Trace the word in the sentence.

I am at home.

Write the word and trace the sentence.

I am at home.

Write the sentence on your own!

I am at home.

 Count the letters in this word. How many does it have?

5

to

Say it, then trace it!

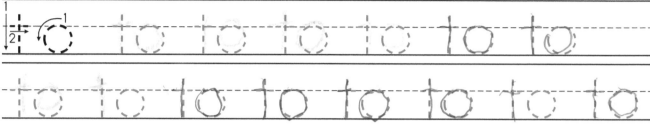

Write the word.

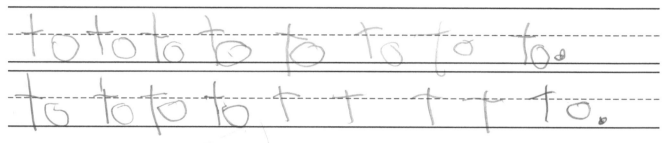

Trace the word in the sentence.

I like to color.

Write the word and trace sentence.

I like to color.

Write the sentence on your own!

I like color.

 Spell this word out loud five times using a baby voice.

in

Say it, then trace it!

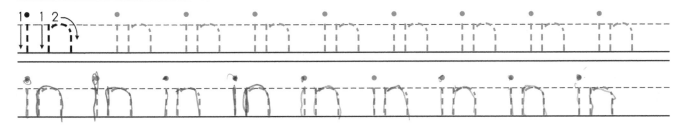

Write the word.

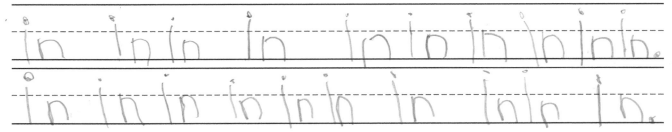

Trace the word in the sentence.

The boat is in the sea.

Write the word and trace the sentence.

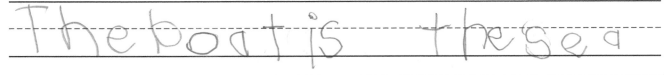
The boat is ___ the sea.

Write the sentence on your own!

The boat is the sea

 Say this word out loud. Can you think of a rhyming word?

is

Say it, then trace it!

is is is is is is is is is is is
is is is is is is is is is is is

Write the word.

is is is is is is is is is is is is is is
is is is is is is is is is is is is is is

Trace the word in the sentence.

The pen is blue.

Write the word and trace the sentence.

The pen is blue.

Write the sentence on your own!

The pen is blue.

 Underline this word on this page every time you see it.

it

Say it, then trace it!

Write the word.

Trace the word in the sentence.

It is raining.

Write the word and trace sentence.

is raining.

Write the sentence on your own!

is raining.

Spell this word out loud. Jump each time you say a letter.

be

Say it, then trace it!

be be be be be be be
be be be be be be be

Write the word.

Trace the word in the sentence.

I want it to be sunny.

Write the word and trace sentence.

I want it to sunny.

Write the sentence on your own!

 Spell this word out loud five times using a whisper voice.

do

Say it, then trace it!

Write the word.

Trace the word in the sentence.

Do you like to jump?

Write the word and trace the sentence.

Do you like to jump?

Write the sentence on your own!

 Find a partner. Take turns spelling this word.

he

Say it, then trace it!

he he he he he he
he he he he he he he

Write the word.

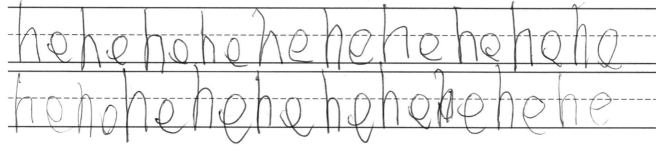

hehehehehehehe
hehehehehehehe

Trace the word in the sentence.

He has two legs.

Write the word and trace the sentence.

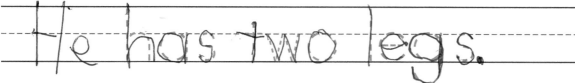

He has two legs.

Write the sentence on your own!

He has two legs.

 Point to each letter and spell the word out loud three times.

no

Say it, then trace it!

no no no no no no no
no no no no no no no

Write the word.

no no no no no no no no no no no
no no no no no no o no no

Trace the word in the sentence.

The balloon has no air.

Write the word and trace sentence.

The balloon has no air.

Write the sentence on your own!

The Balloon has no air.

Spell this word out loud five times using a robot voice.

on

Say it, then trace it!

on on on on on on on

on on on on on on on

Write the word.

Trace the word in the sentence.

A cape is  on his back.

Write the word and trace the sentence.

A cape is his back.

Write the sentence on your own!

 Say each letter while you trace them with your finger.

so

Say it, then trace it!

so so so so so so so so
so so so so so so so so

Write the word.

Trace the word in the sentence.

My jacket is so warm.

Write the word and trace the sentence.

My jacket is warm.

Write the sentence on your own

Think of another word that starts with the same letter.

an

Say it, then trace it!

an an an an an an

an an an an an an

Write the word.

Trace the word in the sentence.

I see an olive.

Write the word and trace the sentence.

I see olive.

Write the sentence on your own!

 Spell this word out loud five times using a singing voice.

as

Say it, then trace it!

as as as as as as as
as as as as as as as

Write the word.

Trace the word in the sentence.

I'm as fast as a tiger.

Write the word and trace the sentence.

I'm ___ fast ___ a tiger.

Write the sentence on your own!

 How many vowels are in this word? (A, E, I, O, U)

by

Say it, then trace it!

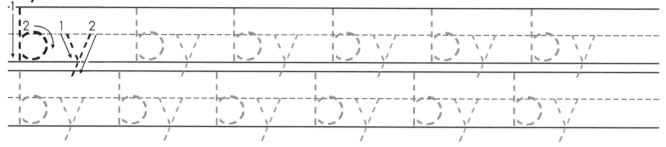

Write the word.

Trace the word in the sentence.

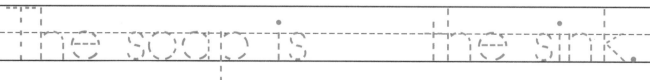

The soap is by the sink.

Write the word and trace the sentence.

The soap is the sink.

Write the sentence on your own!

 How many times can you spell this word in 10 seconds?

of

Say it, then trace it!

Write the word.

Trace the word in the sentence.

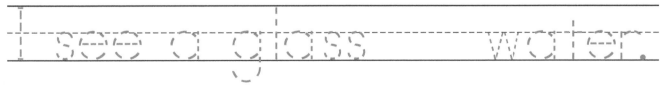

I see a glass of water.

Write the word and trace the sentence.

I see a glass of water.

Write the sentence on your own!

Spell this word out loud five times using a grown-up voice.

am

Say it, then trace it!

am am am am am

am am am am am

Write the word.

Trace the word in the sentence.

I am sad.

Write the word and trace the sentence.

I sad.

Write the sentence on your own!

 Circle this word on this page every time you see it.

if

Say it, then trace it!

Write the word.

Trace the word in the sentence.

See if we have mail.

Write the word and trace the sentence.

Write the sentence on your own!

 Trace over this word five more times with your finger.

up

Say it, then trace it!

up up up up up up
up up up up up up

Write the word.

Trace the word in the sentence.

He is up on the horse.

Write the word and trace sentence.

He is on the horse.

Write the sentence on your own!

 Can you write this word in the air with your finger?

the

Say it, then trace it!

the the the the the the

the the the the the

Write the word.

Trace the word in the sentence.

I see the bear.

Write the word and trace the sentence.

I see bear.

Write the sentence on your own!

 Can you think of another sentence using this word?

can

Say it, then trace it!

c̓a̓n̓ can can can
can can can can can

Write the word.

Trace the word in the sentence.

I can mop the floor.

Write the word and trace the sentence.

I mop the floor.

Write the sentence on your own!

 Spell this word out loud five times using a singing voice.

see

Say it, then trace it!

see see see see see see see see see see see

Write the word.

Trace the word in the sentence.

I see a star.

Write the word and trace the sentence.

I a star.

Write the sentence on your own!

you

Say it, then trace it!

you you you you you
you you you you you

Write the word.

Trace the word in the sentence.

I will wave to you.

Write the word and trace the sentence.

I will wave to

Write the sentence on your own!

 Spell this word out loud five times using a baby voice.

get

Say it, then trace it!

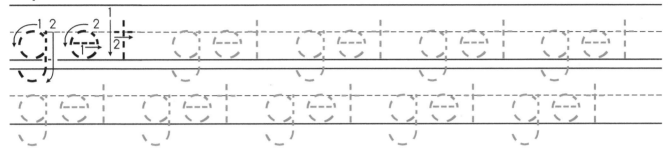

Write the word.

Trace the word in the sentence.

Please get the glue.

Write the word and trace the sentence.

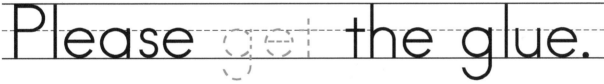

Write the sentence on your own!

Say this word out loud. Can you think of a rhyming word?

27

let

Say it, then trace it!

Write the word.

Trace the word in the sentence.

Let the dog outside.

Write the word and trace the sentence.

the dog outside.

Write the sentence on your own!

 Underline this word on this page every time you see it.

28

all

Say it, then trace it!

all all all all all all all
all all all all all all all

Write the word.

Trace the word in the sentence.

I saved all my money.

Write the word and trace the sentence.

I saved my money.

Write the sentence on your own!

 Spell this word out loud. Jump each time you say a letter.

had

Say it, then trace it!

had had had had
had had had had

Write the word.

Trace the word in the sentence.

I had a pear.

Write the word and trace the sentence.

I_____ a pear.

Write the sentence on your own!

 Spell this word out loud five times using a whisper voice.

has

Say it, then trace it!

has has has has has

has has has has has

Write the word.

Trace the word in the sentence.

The monkey has a tail.

Write the word and trace the sentence.

The monkey _____ a tail.

Write the sentence on your own!

 Find a partner. Take turns spelling this word.

are

Say it, then trace it!

are are are are are

are are are are are

Write the word.

Trace the word in the sentence.

Strawberries are red.

Write the word and trace the sentence.

Strawberries are red.

Write the sentence on your own!

 Point to each letter and spell the word out loud three times.

but

Say it, then trace it!

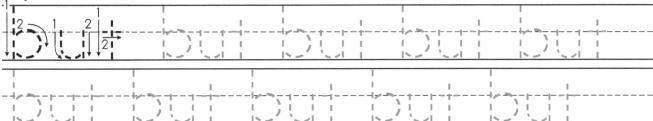

Write the word.

Trace the word in the sentence.

He is small  fast.

Write the word and trace the sentence.

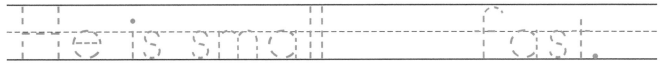

Write the sentence on your own!

 Spell this word out loud five times using a robot voice.

did

Say it, then trace it!

did did did did did
did did did did did

Write the word.

Trace the word in the sentence.

Did you see a crab?

Write the word and trace the sentence.

you see a crab?

Write the sentence on your own!

 Say each letter while you trace them with your finger.

34

now

Say it, then trace it!

1 2 1 1 2 3 4
now now now now
now now now now

Write the word.

Trace the word in the sentence.

It is time to go now.

Write the word and trace the sentence.

It is time to go   .

Write the sentence on your own!

 Spell this word out loud five times using a singing voice.

out

Say it, then trace it!

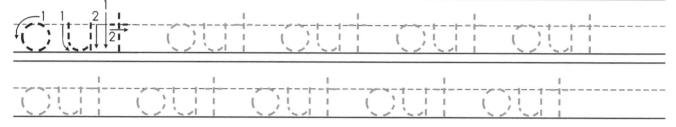

Write the word.

Trace the word in the sentence.

I am out of the bath.

Write the word and trace the sentence.

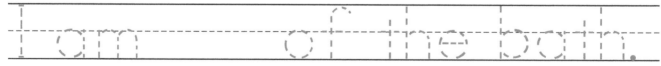

Write the sentence on your own!

 Say this word out loud. Can you think of a rhyming word?

she

Say it, then trace it!

she she she she she
she she she she she

Write the word.

Trace the word in the sentence.

She is a mom.

Write the word and trace the sentence.

_____ is a mom.

Write the sentence on your own!

 How many vowels are in this word? (A, E, I, O, U)

37

was

Say it, then trace it!

¹ ² ³ ⁴ was ⁻¹ ² ¹
was   was   was   was

was   was   was   was   was

Write the word.

Trace the word in the sentence.

The fan was on.

Write the word and trace the sentence.

The fan   on.

Write the sentence on your own!

 How many times can you spell this word in 10 seconds?

who

Say it, then trace it!

1 2 3 4 who who who who

who who who who who

Write the word.

Trace the word in the sentence.

Who likes ice cream?

Write the word and trace the sentence.

likes ice cream?

Write the sentence on your own!

 Spell this word out loud five times using a grown-up voice.

her

Say it, then trace it!

her her her her her

her her her her her

Write the word.

Trace the word in the sentence.

Her coat is yellow.

Write the word and trace the sentence.

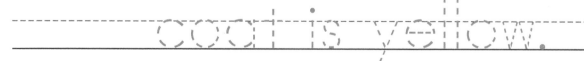

coat is yellow.

Write the sentence on your own!

Circle this word on this page every time you see it.

him

Say it, then trace it!

him him him him him

him him him him him

Write the word.

Trace the word in the sentence.

I am with him.

Write the word and trace the sentence.

I am with

Write the sentence on your own!

 Trace over this word five more times with your finger.

his

Say it, then trace it!

his his his his his his
his his his his his his his

Write the word.

Trace the word in the sentence.

His shell is green.

Write the word and trace the sentence.

shell is green.

Write the sentence on your own!

 Can you write this word in the air with your finger?

how

Say it, then trace it!

how how how how
how how how how how

Write the word.

Trace the word in the sentence.

How much is it?

Write the word and trace the sentence.

much is it?

Write the sentence on your own!

 Can you think of another sentence using this word?

43

may

Say it, then trace it!

may may may may
may may may may

Write the word.

Trace the word in the sentence.

It may be cloudy out.

Write the word and trace the sentence.

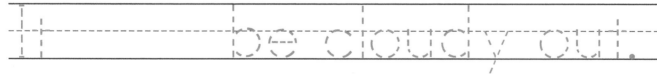

Write the sentence on your own!

 Spell this word out loud. Clap each time you say a letter.

eat

Say it, then trace it!

eat eat eat eat eat

eat eat eat eat eat

Write the word.

Trace the word in the sentence.

I like to eat pizza.

Write the word and trace the sentence.

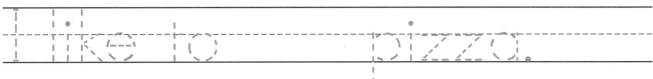

I like to   pizza.

Write the sentence on your own!

Count the letters in this word. How many does it have?

45

new

Say it, then trace it!

new new new new

new new new new

Write the word.

Trace the word in the sentence.

I have a new yo-yo.

Write the word and trace sentence.

I have a yo-yo.

Write the sentence on your own!

 Spell this word out loud five times using a baby voice.

saw

Say it, then trace it!

saw saw saw saw

saw saw saw saw saw

Write the word.

Trace the word in the sentence.

She saw a unicorn.

Write the word and trace the sentence.

She a unicorn.

Write the sentence on your own!

 Say this word out loud. Can you think of a rhyming word?

say

Say it, then trace it!

say say say say say
say say say say say

Write the word.

Trace the word in the sentence.

I can say my name.

Write the word and trace sentence.

I can ___ my name.

Write the sentence on your own!

 Underline this word on this page every time you see it.

ran

Say it, then trace it!

ran ran ran ran ran

ran ran ran ran ran

Write the word.

Trace the word in the sentence.

He ran fast.

Write the word and trace the sentence.

He fast.

Write the sentence on your own!

 Spell this word out loud. Jump each time you say a letter.

yes

Say it, then trace it!

yes yes yes yes yes
yes yes yes yes yes

Write the word.

Trace the word in the sentence.

I say yes to cupcakes!

Write the word and trace sentence.

I say _____ to cupcakes.

Write the sentence on your own!

 Spell this word out loud five times using a whisper voice.

way

Say it, then trace it!

way way way way
way way way way

Write the word.

Trace the word in the sentence.

A train is on the way.

Write the word and trace the sentence.

A train is on the _____.

Write the sentence on your own!

 Find a partner. Take turns spelling this word.

day

Say it, then trace it!

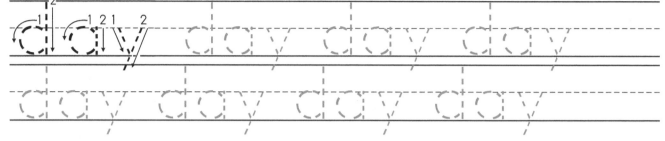

Write the word.

Trace the word in the sentence.

It is a hot day.

Write the word and trace the sentence.

Write the sentence on your own!

 Point to each letter and spell the word out loud three times.

get

Say it, then trace it!

get get get get get
get get get get get

Write the word.

Trace the word in the sentence.

Please get the tape.

Write the word and trace the sentence.

Please the tape.

Write the sentence on your own!

 Spell this word out loud five times using a robot voice.

and

Say it, then trace it!

and and and and and
and and and and

Write the word.

Trace the word in the sentence.

Bees buzz and fly.

Write the word and trace the sentence.

Bees buzz fly.

Write the sentence on your own!

 Say each letter while you trace them with your finger.

for

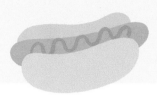

Say it, then trace it!

for for for for for for

for for for for for for

Write the word.

Trace the word in the sentence.

The hot dog is for me.

Write the word and trace the sentence.

The hot dog is me.

Write the sentence on your own!

 Think of another word that starts with the same letter.

put

Say it, then trace it!

put put put put put
put put put put put

Write the word.

Trace the word in the sentence.

I put the cart away.

Write the word and trace the sentence.

Write the sentence on your own!

 Underline this word on this page every time you see it.

56

not

Say it, then trace it!

not not not not not
not not not not not

Write the word.

Trace the word in the sentence.

I did not hear you.

Write the word and trace the sentence.

I did not hear you.

Write the sentence on your own!

How many vowels are in this word? (A, E, I, O, U)

ask

Say it, then trace it!

ask ask ask ask ask

ask ask ask ask ask

Write the word.

Trace the word in the sentence.

I will ask my dad.

Write the word and trace the sentence.

I will my dad.

Write the sentence on your own!

 Count the letters in this word. How many does it have?

like

Say it, then trace it!

l i k e   like   like   like   like

like   like   like   like

Write the word.

Trace the word in the sentence.

I like to kick the ball.

Write the word and trace the sentence.

I _____ to kick the ball.

Write the sentence on your own!

 Spell this word out loud five times using a grown-up voice.

have

Say it, then trace it!

have have have
have have have have

Write the word.

Trace the word in the sentence.

We have a gate.

Write the word and trace the sentence.

We a gate.

Write the sentence on your own!

 Circle this word on this page every time you see it.

look

Say it, then trace it!

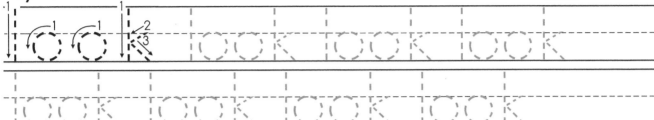

Write the word.

Trace the word in the sentence.

look at the rocket!

Write the word and trace the sentence.

Write the sentence on your own!

Trace over this word five more times with your finger.

said

Say it, then trace it!

said said said said

said said said said

Write the word.

Trace the word in the sentence.

I said to go to bed.

Write the word and trace the sentence.

I to go to bed.

Write the sentence on your own!

 Can you write this word in the air with your finger?

want

Say it, then trace it!

1 2 3 4 1 2 1 2 1
2

~~want want want~~

~~want want want want~~

Write the word.

Trace the word in the sentence.

I ~~want~~ some bacon.

Write the word and trace the sentence.

I ~~some bacon.~~

Write the sentence on your own!

 Can you think of another sentence using this word?

went

Say it, then trace it!

went went went went
went went went went

Write the word.

Trace the word in the sentence.

We went on a plane.

Write the word and trace the sentence.

We on a plane.

Write the sentence on your own!

 Spell this word out loud. Clap each time you say a letter.

64

that

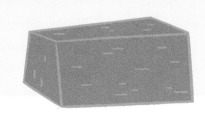

Say it, then trace it!

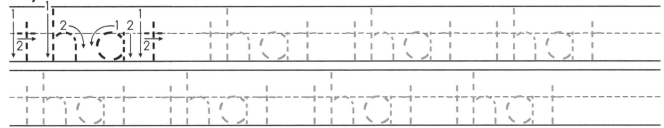

Write the word.

Trace the word in the sentence.

 brick is heavy.

Write the word and trace the sentence.

Write the sentence on your own!

 Count the letters in this word. How many does it have?

they

Say it, then trace it!

they they they they
they they they they

Write the word.

Trace the word in the sentence.

They won the game!

Write the word and trace the sentence.

won the game!

Write the sentence on your own!

 Spell this word out loud five times using a baby voice.

this

Say it, then trace it!

this this this this this
this this this this this

Write the word.

Trace the word in the sentence.

Can I wear this ring?

Write the word and trace the sentence.

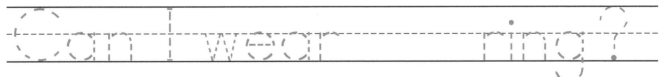

Write the sentence on your own!

 Say this word out loud. Can you think of a rhyming word?

what

Say it, then trace it!

Write the word.

Trace the word in the sentence.

What **do pirates like?**

Write the word and trace the sentence.

Write the sentence on your own!

 Underline this word on this page every time you see it.

will

Say it, then trace it!

1 2 3 4 1

will will will will will will
will will will will will will

Write the word.

Trace the word in the sentence.

The kite will fly.

Write the word and trace the sentence.

The kite fly.

Write the sentence on your own!

 Spell this word out loud. Jump each time you say a letter.

with

Say it, then trace it!

1 2 3 4 with with with with

with with with with with

Write the word.

Trace the word in the sentence.

He smiles with joy.

Write the word and trace the sentence.

He smiles joy.

Write the sentence on your own!

 Spell this word out loud five times using a whisper voice.

from

Say it, then trace it!

from from from from
from from from

Write the word.

Trace the word in the sentence.

Shells are from the sea.

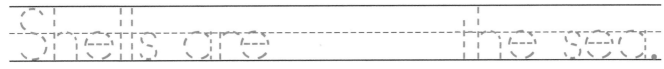

Write the word and trace the sentence.

Shells are the sea.

Write the sentence on your own!

Find a partner. Take turns spelling this word.

71

some

Say it, then trace it!

some some some

some some some

Write the word.

Trace the word in the sentence.

I need some jam.

Write the word and trace the sentence.

I need jam.

Write the sentence on your own!

 Point to each letter and spell the word out loud three times.

them

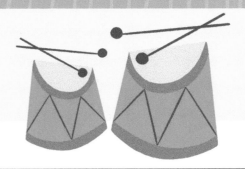

Say it, then trace it!

them them them
them them them

Write the word.

Trace the word in the sentence.

I can beat them.

Write the word and trace the sentence.

I can beat

Write the sentence on your own!

 Spell this word out loud five times using a robot voice.

then

Say it, then trace it!

Write the word.

Trace the word in the sentence.

Swing, then hit the ball.

Write the word and trace the sentence.

Write the sentence on your own!

 Say each letter while you trace them with your finger.

were

Say it, then trace it!

1 2 3 4 2 1 2 2
were were were were
were were were were

Write the word.

Trace the word in the sentence.

The snails were slow.

Write the word and trace the sentence.

The snails   slow.

Write the sentence on your own!

Think of another word that starts with the same letter.

when

Say it, then trace it!

when when when
when when when

Write the word.

Trace the word in the sentence.

When is my birthday?

Write the word and trace the sentence.

is my birthday?

Write the sentence on your own!

 Spell this word out loud. Clap each time you say a letter.

just

Say it, then trace it!

just just just just just
just just just just just

Write the word.

Trace the word in the sentence.

She is just a baby.

Write the word and trace the sentence.

She is a baby.

Write the sentence on your own!

 How many vowels are in this word? (A, E, I, O, U)

live

Say it, then trace it!

live live live live live
live live live live live

Write the word.

Trace the word in the sentence.

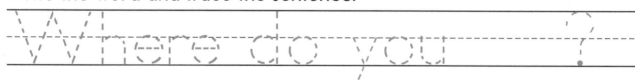

Where do you live?

Write the word and trace the sentence.

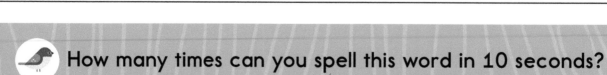

Where do you ___?

Write the sentence on your own!

How many times can you spell this word in 10 seconds?

play

Say it, then trace it!

play play play play
play play play play

Write the word.

Trace the word in the sentence.

I can play soccer.

Write the word and trace the sentence.

I can soccer.

Write the sentence on your own!

 Spell this word out loud five times using a grown-up voice.

79

open

Say it, then trace it!

open open open
open open open

Write the word.

Trace the word in the sentence.

I will open the lock.

Write the word and trace the sentence.

I will the lock.

Write the sentence on your own!

 Circle this word on this page every time you see it.

80

take

Say it, then trace it!

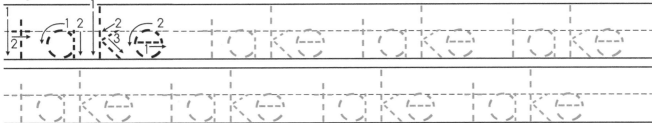

Write the word.

Trace the word in the sentence.

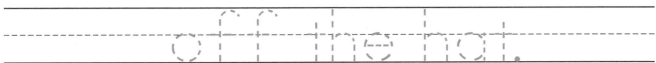
Take off the hat.

Write the word and trace the sentence.

Write the sentence on your own!

 Trace over this word five more times with your finger.

ride

Say it, then trace it!

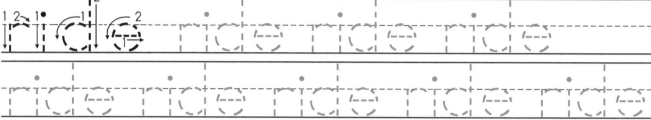

Write the word.

Trace the word in the sentence.

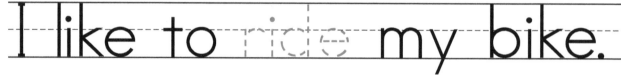

I like to ride my bike.

Write the word and trace the sentence.

I like to my bike.

Write the sentence on your own!

Can you write this word in the air with your finger?

well

Say it, then trace it!

1 2 3 4 2
well well well well well
well well well well well

Write the word.

Trace the word in the sentence.

The eagle can fly well.

Write the word and trace the sentence.

The eagle can fly.

Write the sentence on your own!

 Can you think of another sentence using this word?

83

your

Say it, then trace it!

your your your your
your your your your

Write the word.

Trace the word in the sentence.

Here is your phone.

Write the word and trace the sentence.

Here is phone.

Write the sentence on your own!

 Spell this word out loud. Clap each time you say a letter.

84

make

Say it, then trace it!

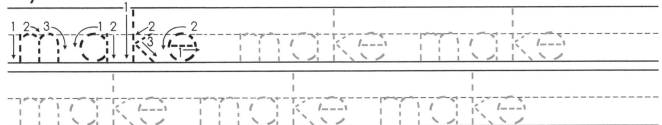

Write the word.

Trace the word in the sentence.

I can make a castle.

Write the word and trace the sentence.

Write the sentence on your own!

 Count the letters in this word. How many does it have?

more

Say it, then trace it!

more more more

more more more

Write the word.

Trace the word in the sentence.

Can I eat more bread?

Write the word and trace the sentence.

Can I eat more bread?

Write the sentence on your own!

 Spell this word out loud five times using a baby voice.

find

Say it, then trace it!

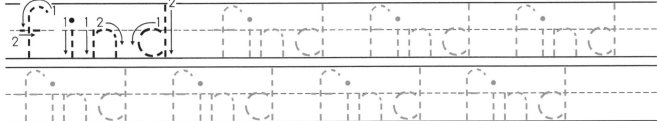

Write the word.

Trace the word in the sentence.

I need to find a plug.

Write the word and trace the sentence.

Write the sentence on your own!

 Spell this word out loud five times using a singing voice.

down

Say it, then trace it!

down down down
down down down

Write the word.

Trace the word in the sentence.

I want to sit down.

Write the word and trace the sentence.

I want to sit .

Write the sentence on your own!

 Underline this word on this page every time you see it.

88

come

Say it, then trace it!

come come come

come come come

Write the word.

Trace the word in the sentence.

Come see the rainbow.

Write the word and trace the sentence.

_____ see the rainbow.

Write the sentence on your own!

 Spell this word out loud. Jump each time you say a letter.

made

Say it, then trace it!

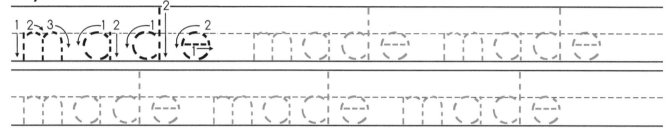

Write the word.

Trace the word in the sentence.

The pig 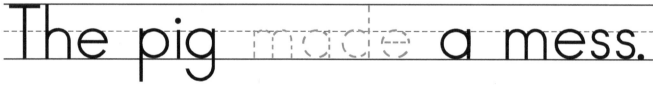 a mess.

Write the word and trace the sentence.

Write the sentence on your own!

 Spell this word out loud five times using a whisper voice.

good

Say it, then trace it!

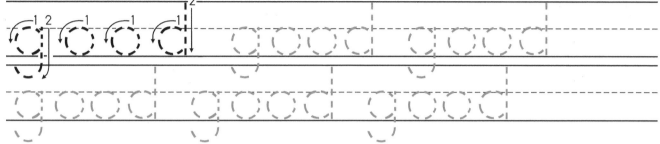

Write the word.

Trace the word in the sentence.

Broccoli is good for me.

Write the word and trace the sentence.

Broccoli is for me.

Write the sentence on your own!

 Find a partner. Take turns spelling this word.

91

give

Say it, then trace it!

give give give give give
give give give give

Write the word.

Trace the word in the sentence.

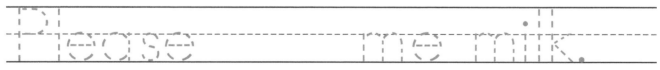
Please give me milk.

Write the word and trace the sentence.

Please me milk.

Write the sentence on your own!

Point to each letter and spell the word out loud three times.

into

Say it, then trace it!

into into into into into into

into into into into into into

Write the word.

Trace the word in the sentence.

It goes into the box.

Write the word and trace the sentence.

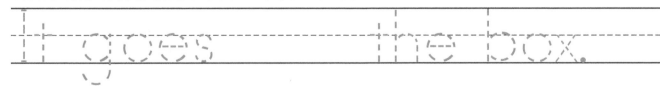
It goes _____ the box.

Write the sentence on your own!

Think of another word that starts with the same letter.

there

Say it, then trace it!

there there there there
there there there

Write the word.

Trace the word in the sentence.

There is a mountain!

Write the word and trace the sentence.

is a mountain!

Write the sentence on your own!

 Say each letter while you trace them with your finger.

after

Say it, then trace it!

after after after
after after after

Write the word.

Trace the word in the sentence.

I ate grapes after pie.

Write the word and trace the sentence.

I ate grapes pie.

Write the sentence on your own!

 Count the letters in this word. How many does it have?

could

Say it, then trace it!

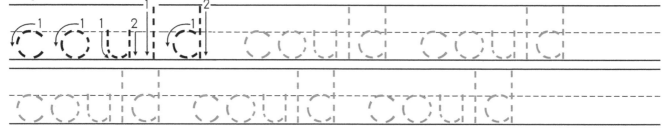

Write the word.

Trace the word in the sentence.

The frog could hop.

Write the word and trace the sentence.

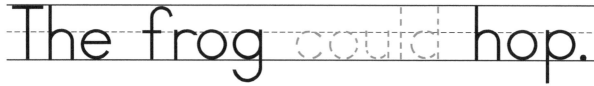
The frog hop.

Write the sentence on your own!

Spell this word out loud five times using a singing voice.

96

every

Say it, then trace it!

every every every
every every every

Write the word.

Trace the word in the sentence.

I like every bug.

Write the word and trace the sentence.

I like bug.

Write the sentence on your own!

 How many vowels are in this word? (A, E, I, O, U)

97

going

Say it, then trace it!

going going going
going going going

Write the word.

Trace the word in the sentence.

I am going on a boat.

Write the word and trace the sentence.

I am on a boat.

Write the sentence on your own!

 How many times can you spell this word in 10 seconds?

thank

Say it, then trace it!

thank thank thank

thank thank thank

Write the word.

Trace the word in the sentence.

I will thank the queen.

Write the word and trace the sentence.

I will the queen.

Write the sentence on your own!

 Spell this word out loud five times using a grown-up voice.

please

Say it, then trace it!

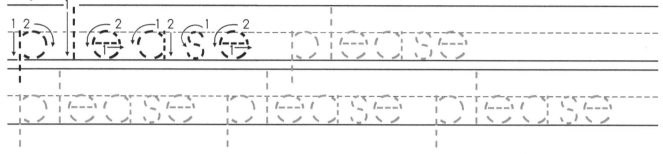

Write the word.

Trace the word in the sentence.

Please get a pencil.

Write the word and trace the sentence.

get a pencil.

Write the sentence on your own!

 Circle this word on this page every time you see it.

100

pretty

Say it, then trace it!

pretty pretty pretty

pretty pretty pretty

Write the word.

Trace the word in the sentence.

The flower is pretty.

Write the word and trace the sentence.

The flower is

Write the sentence on your own!

You did it!

certificate
of completion

Congratulations on
completing all 100 words!
You are a STAR!

Sign your name below:

_____

Date: _____

CPSIA information can be obtained
at www.ICGtesting.com
Printed in the USA
JSHW040510180620
6263JS00005B/41